Ledge

Ledge
Nola Garrett

Mayapple Press 2016

Copyright © 2016 by Nola Garrett

Published by Mayapple Press
              362 Chestnut Hill Road
              Woodstock, NY 12498
              mayapplepress.com

ISBN 978-1-936419--68-5
Library of Congress Control Number: 2016909592

ACKNOWLEDGEMENTS

I am grateful to the editors of the following publications where these poems, some under different titles, first appeared.

Able Muse: Forty Years Later; *American Poets & Poetry:* Elegy for John Ciardi; *Christian Century:* Absurd, January 26th: the Anniversary of My Mother's Death, Lillian, Althea, Hattie, Zada, Neutral Ground, Testaments; *coalhillreview.com*: Dyeing; *Crab Orchard Review:* Aubade, The Relative Heart; *823 on High*: Neutral Ground, Paraphasia; *Field:* Alligator Regrets the Anhinga, Alligator Reasons a World View; *Georgia Review:* The Pastor's Wife Considers Her Chops; *Imagination & Place:* French Creek; *Pittsburgh Post-Gazette:* Copper Crayola; *The Strip:* Jimmy; *Voices from the Attic:* The Pastor's Ex-wife's Compline.

"Decoration Day" was reprinted in *Obsession: Sestinas in the Twenty-First Century*, Ed. Carolyn Beard Whitlow and Marilyn Krysl, Darmouth College Press, 2014. "My Friend Melissa" was published in *The Muse Strikes Back: A Poetic Response by Women to Men*. Ed. Katherine McAlpine & Gail White. Story Line Press, 1997. Selected Poems from *The Dynamite Maker's Mistress* (2009) David Robert Books.

I will always be indebted to Leonard Trawick who taught me to write my first sestina and to Yaddo where I was given the time to explore the sestina form.

I remain appreciative to Edinboro Universtiy of PA for ongoing support.

I have been blessed with first readers, poetry friends, and family members past and present who have shaped the new poems within this collection. Thank you Mercyhurst Community Poetry Workshop, Anne Rashid, The Mad Women in the Attic, Mike Simms, Patricia Callan, Nick Samaras, Kim Bridgford, Judith Kerman, Ronald Garrett, Natasha Garrett, Channing Garrett, and Alfred Garrett.

Cover design by Judith Kerman; cover photo courtesy of Spencer Morrissey. (Please visit Facebook page for Spencer Morrissey Photographer.) Photo of author by Lifetouch. Book designed and typeset by Amee Schmidt with titles in Baskerville Old Face and text in Calisto MT.

Contents

I

The Pastor's Wife Considers Her Chops	7
Testaments	8
Copper Crayola	9
The Relative Heart	10
My Friend Melissa	11
Absurd	13
Elegy for John Ciardi	14
Jimmy	15
Dyeing	17
Lillian, Althea, Hattie, Zada	19
January 26th: the Anniversary of My Mother's Death	20
Forty Years Later	21
French Creek	22

II

Limestone Karst	27
Incontinence	28
Alligator Regrets the Anhinga	30
Alligator Orders the Animal Powers Meditation Kit	31
Alligator Reasons a World View	32
Ledge	33
Aubade	34
Paraphasia	35
Inadmissible Evidence	37
Neutral Ground	39
Irretrievably Broken	40
Relief	41
The Pastor's Ex-wife's Compline	42
Prayer for My Last Husband's New Wife	43

Selected Poems

Landscape with Six Plastic Flamingos	47
Decoration Day	49
Gong	51
False Aralia	53
Kohl	54
Courier	56
The Dynamite Maker's Mistress	58
Hosea Three	60
Gomer 60	
Hosea 62	
Yahweh 64	
At the Corner of Hoover and Sparkleberry	66
Mahjongg	68
Janet Reno's Poinciana Tree	70
The Pastor's Wife Considers Her 57th Birthday	72
Four Residents	74
Apple Hearts for Sylvia Plath 74	
Getting up, Leaving 76	
Hats, Fans, Coffins, Boats 77	
Letter Home 79	
Perchance, Each Interstate	81
The Pastor's Wife Considers	
the Retirement of Fred the Magician	83
Elegy for Anthony Hecht	85
A Cadenza for Arnaut Daniel	87
About the Author	89

For
Stefanie Small, who has seen me through my darkest time—thank you.

I

Batter my heart, three-personed God; for You
as yet but knock, breathe, shine, and seek to mend:
    Holy Sonnet XIV l. 1,2
    John Donne

The Pastor's Wife Considers Her Chops

I come from a long line of butchers, called
to slaughter hogs, steers, dry milk cows
on the hay mow side of bank barns
where the animals never go.
                              I prize knives,
mallets, surprise, spare words.
I saw. I slice. I trim. I discard. I
rearrange body parts. I will grind
anything for the sake of tenderness.

Testaments

Isaac Tells Rebecca

It was bad enough my old man was so old
and wandered. One Sabbath
instead of leading the sheep,
he forgot and made me carry the wood.
Just like always he got out his father's knife,
blew on that little punk flame, looked up;
and then I knew he thought
I was the lamb.
O my God! I screamed.
He seemed dazed, but he finally found a ram.

All my life I've been his son.

Jesus Tells Mary Magdalene

It's strange enough my dad is so old
and wonders
how to make everything different.
One Sunday instead of dinner
he sent me out to Nazareth.
Just like always he made the face,
the belly, the little hands with fingernails.
He said that I am the lamb.
O my god! I cried,
but he seemed pleased
he'd found a new way.

Copper Crayola

The price of copper is going up!
I've heard all my life: first

from my Dad who'd trade
meat, cheese, the use of his truck
for a secondhand pound or two:

old plumbing, wire, roofing, a still;

then, from my son who scrounges
abandoned houses, dumpsters,
under bridges, Pittsburgh streets:

car parts, bracelets, a weather vane.

Now, while I read the news
my grandson sits next to me
coloring with his prize crayon:

pennies, a rooster, and the wheels
on a bus going round and round.

The Relative Heart

My great-great-grandfather Enos Thompson assassinated
a high-ranking member of the Know Nothing Party,
then retreated to California. My family said his stories
of giant redwoods, painted deserts,
and mountains so high trees wouldn't grow
made politics seem unimportant.

Grandpa Weed was a certified chicken thief,
spent 30 days (along with Uncle Morris)
in the Crawford County Jail to make it official.
All my uncles said *that* farmer misunderstood the deal,
and besides The Depression was hard times.

Cousin Bob was found in a field naked from the waist down
in a compromising position with a chestnut mare.
My relatives were grateful it wasn't a stallion or worse—
a gelding—so it wasn't a completely unnatural act.

My second cousin, Bruce, on my mother's side,
shot his daddy (who beat him regularly) and then his mom
(after she complained) with a .22,
because they wouldn't let him wear blue jeans.
The family maintains he solved all his problems
and some of theirs now that he's required to wear denim.

My third cousin once removed took her husband's life insurance
and finally got to travel. Cousin Lola
was the first white woman to spend the winter
in Point Barrow, Alaska, and the last to leave a Greyhound bus
where she had quietly died at the age of 89.

Uncle Otis drank himself to death, served
as an example to my father who never touched a drop.
My brother, Joel, one fresh June morning on a dare
chug-a-lugged a fifth of vodka, lay down
and died in the bed of his pick-up truck. My mother
still remarks how heart trouble runs all through this family.

My Friend Melissa

after Charles Causley's "My Friend Maloney"

My friend Melissa, eighteen,
Smokes like a chimney,
Ran into trouble two years back
With the local gentry.

Pastor and mayor's sons
Climbed atop her.
The psychologist took one look at Melissa,
Fixed her proper,

Talked of the crime of youth,
The innocent victim.
Melissa never said a kind word
To contradict him.

Melissa of French Street,
Back of the City Mission,
Daughter of a crack pusher,
Blamed television.

Psychotherapy triumphed.
Everyone felt fine.
Things went deader.
Melissa reeled in her line.

Melissa lost a thing or two
Changing orientation.
First skirt, second innocence,
The old irresolution.

Found herself a girl-friend,
Sharp hair, drab colors.
Melissa drives a Volvo,
Sued for one million dollars.

College boys on the corner
Polish their black Blazers,
Look at old Melissa,
Eyes like dull razors.

"I don't need hassle," says Melissa.
My partner is a fox.
What you're not, she's got, fellers.
You can keep your mean cocks."

Pastor got a TV show,
Mayor, in the end the same.
The psychologist incorporated.
"Life," said Melissa, "is a game."

Consider then the case of Melissa,
College boys, pastor, mayor, shrink.
Who was the victor and who was the victim?
Think.

Absurd

1.

I don't go to Johnnie Arnone's
Italian Delicatessen often.
Johnnie, round and ageless, stands pleased
amidst his piled angel hair pasta,
olive oil, pizzelles, and hanging mozzarella;
presses on me samples of salami
and antipasto salad and says "Taste
the provolone and take this sub home
for the mister," and I'm thanking
and protesting and mentioning profit
and he's adding too few numbers
and an extra loaf of bread, and I'm not even
Italian. Who on earth does Johnnie think
he is? God? Giving away the bread!

2.

What we're made of sometimes
is calculated in calcium, iron,
and phosphorus whose worth
inflates each year. Each body, an investment,
accumulates cucumbers, artichokes,
a pinch of salt, garlic, tomatoes,
Thanksgiving, gooseberry fool, and hot sausage
sandwiches with fried green peppers and onions
on homemade Italian rolls
                            now baked by Sylvie,
Johnny Arnone's widow, who wears
a shapeless black dress and still cries, *because
it's only been a year and it's baseball season
and Johnny could have been a catcher
for the New York Yankees, but he stayed home,
since his father, too, died young, and
everybody counted on Johnny to start
the tomatoes, the peppers and the cucumbers.*

Elegy for John Ciardi

John Ciardi died last Sunday night—officially
myocardial infarction—but I believe
he was wrestling a couplet into place
so you'd not notice the rhyme until after
you'd been surprised by the meaning,
and the heft of one word's history was just
too much. Dante and Beatrice stopped by
to help. "Just returning a favorite metaphor.
Use it for leverage," said the travelers.
And with that Ciardi knew how his poem
meant, and his last couplet slammed shut
in sweetest freshness, healed of winter's scars;
perfiect, pure and ready for the stars.

Jimmy

Though you'd call me homeless, my city,
Pittsburgh, is my clean,
well-lighted place I know must change.
Though I drink Jack Daniel, I don't do crack.
In the pot, Mom, you gave me, I perk coffee,
sharpen my dull nights and my neon

days, crossing the 16th St. Bridge to The Strip's neon
green cabbage mountains that feed my city
that still lives on golupki, bread, and coffee
laid out for workmen, clean
out of work that won't be back 'til the Crack
of Doom. No more changing

a pour of coke and ore into steel changed
again into girders. Now, we make neon
robots, learn to fix hearts, concoct crack-
proof glass—our recipes for a city
that employs its ketchup factory as lofts for coffee
sippers. Thursdays, I clean

their homes: dust their trophies, clean
their windows, gather their loose change
from their carpets. I'm their coffee-
stained, weird man amid their lit neon
liqueur ware. I'm the tattooed city
guy who drives home to a borrowed room, cracks

a beer, eats canned corned beef hash, cracks
a philosophy book now and then. Good clean
fun mostly. Fridays, I pick up Baylie at her city
elementary school on the South Side, change
into the Daddy who will draw flowers with her neon
pencil, buy her milk and berries, sneak her sips of coffee

when she teases me. She giggles her coffee
breath all over me. Mom, how am I going to crack
into a real job? How can I trade my drawings of neon
flowers for the money to buy my own house to clean,
a place you and Baylie can visit me? Change
me? I don't think so. Where's the key to my city?

Dyeing

1.

I never saw my grandmother twice
with the same colored hair.
Instead of the world, she traveled the spectrum—
Tahitian Brown, Romanian Gold, Irish Red—
without even the pretense of reclaiming
tints once hers.
              I was so embarrassed,
my teenaged self nearly died.

My grandmother after years of misdiagnosis
died. Rather than her liver,
it was her heart after all,
                      but who could tell?
As for myself, one October afternoon
when an early snow on my unraked leaves
looked like me peering out of my mirror
at an old self, I wasn't quite ready. Yet,
my staid self departed on Light Brown #7.

2.

During my afternoon walk, I may have found
a geode. Gray, hunched, a little off-center
it could be opened, perhaps to a scatter of sand
or to an amethyst vault,
                    or left alone
like both my grandmothers. Oh, they married,
raised their share of children, but as widows
their lives began.
                Neither was a *Mrs.*—
Just Belle and Marie.
                    Belle for a living
sewed and mended, reused her basting thread,
played church piano, read, bathed at her kitchen sink
with multi-colored soap slivers.
                          Marie watched

TV evangelists, favored her richest son, dyed her hair
a different color every month, window shopped daily,
preferred rhinestones and orange.

Disliking dogs, sticky children and old men,
Belle and Marie each slept away
in their small lavender rooms.
I smile. I whisper back to them
my middle name—Maribel.

Lillian, Althea, Hattie, Zada

Praise all folds, crinkles, gathers,
pleats both sharp and rumpled,
corrugated cardboard's columned smocking.

Praise sun-dried blue jeans and raisins'
ancient sweetness: old hymns'
complex thought clothed in easy rhymes.

Praise creases: English walnuts:
each human brain dreaming a future
while claiming the past. Now, praise
time's thousand cranes: wrinkles
and grandmothers' recycled names.

January 26th: the Anniversary of My Mother's Death

He is green before the sun,
and his branch shooteth forth
in his garden.
      —Job 8:16

Today, I am five years older than she was.
Mom didn't have time to tell me everything.

All my green chairs were my mother's,
who inherited hers from God knows where.

Because some green chairs never wear out,
I wish I could know everything about green:

nature's timeless neutral, algae, fir trees,
grasses, fronds, the peacock's iridescence:

some dragons, most jade, copper's verdigris,
oil of sage, chrysoprase, and sunset's moment—

the green flash—Yahweh's infinity wand.

Forty Years Later

Why bother to root for my brother Joel?
Surely, your quarterback's body is earth's, Joel.

You knew how to sell elaborate jokes—
seemingly, you stand at my door grinning, Joel.

Named for the prophet of locusts and *kairos*,
has the Lord dealt wondrously with you, Joel?

Our mother was a saver of used things
that someday would be useful; she wept, Joel.

I could not have borne following your hearse
through rain. You were buried in sunlight, Joel.

Cocoa, Monopoly, the school bus
we shared. Without you I grow older, Joel.

Ten minutes! You chugged a fifth of vodka,
celebrating your last truck payment, Joel.

No *la ,ti, do* for you, your radio blasted.
You've passed the reach of all devices, Joel.

French Creek

> *Springs are fed by rain and rain alone.*
> *—Benard Palissy*

Up north from Florida, here on the bank I stand
where French Creek winds through the dandelion

plantations of my mind. Though some say *creek*,
others *crick*, every spring someone drowns.

Drop offs. French Creek's holes hide where scraps of rock
whorled depressions. Only the stones and their places

have changed, not French Creek. Beneath their yellow
slickers our volunteer firemen pale, carry

up the creek's bank the sagging, green body bags:
the Watsons' girl, whole canoes of Boy Scouts,

and Eli Yovich swimming after dark with
his girl friend. Later, his thin-lipped wife

took over the fruit and vegetable stand
he used to run down by Pollick's Bridge.

She raised his prices, bickered with my Aunt Martha
about Decoration Day geraniums until

Aunt Martha never went back.
Beside the creek this spring the stand leans empty.

Glaciers have been here and may come again,
creep up on us the way they have crept up

on Gilbert Stuart's portrait of Washington.
The work of glaciers is abrasion. Chalk on

slate they rewrite the land, the rivers. Some
say before the last Ice Age, the Allegheny

flowed to Lake Erie through French Creek's
present channel. When ice masses blocked

the river's northern escape, its flow reversed.
Now French Creek runs south west, meanders,

braids, has it both ways, unlike us
schooled beneath George Washington's cool gaze.

For one so old, how fresh he always seemed
from where I sat in sixth grade with Mr. Culbertson

who read from Parkman what we ought to know
about our swimming hole's place in history:

*The surrounding forests had dropped their leaves
in gray and patient desolation. Chill*

rains drizzled the clearings. Bison fed.
Le Boeuf the French called them and then

the creek, too—*Riviere aux Boeuf*—as if
the river were a beast wandering to where

it nudged the Allegheny at Venango—
their meeting place—though meeting with the French

was all that young George Washington could bear.
I cannot say that ever in my life

*have I suffered so much anxiety
as I did in this affair.... French Creek*

is a very crooked river. He wrote
in his diary as if the creek, *their* river,

were the grinning French who would not treaty,
who waved him back down stream that grim December

in 1753, loaded his canoes
with barrels of cheap French brandy—Indian lure.

23

Old willows ached over the lee meanders,
chill rain drizzled the clearings. In gray

and patient desolation snow fell. Ice formed.
Floes tossed, cracked casks, spilling our father's wine

down French Creek, the Allegheny, the Ohio,
the Mississippi past all plantations,

out to the Gulf of Mexico to rain
returning, like me, to French Creek—home.

II

Yet dearly I love You, would be loved fain,
….
Divorce me, untie or break that knot again,
  Holy Sonnet XIV l. 9, 11
  John Donne

Limestone Karst

> *The good life is being able to live*
> *through moments of losing yourself.*
>   *—Henry Moore*

I live on the west bank of Lake St. George,
a collapsed sink hole, whose steep muck banks
settle into the basin holding them. I know

over geologic time all lakes are temporary.
This morning's south wind arrives like a tow truck
pulling the lake's surface north, while an undercurrent

wears away my lake's sides. Beneath
my lake's sediment lies a faithless clay bed,
ready at any moment to fall into the arms

and crevices of a limestone karst, drunken
host of the Florida aquifer. Yet, like the diving
anhingas or the shrieking ospreys, I feel at home.

Incontinence

Ruth Eckerd Concert Hall

Stefan Sanderling poles Sibelius' raft, *En Saga*, into fiordless
Clearwater, FL. Violins and oboes

take turns. Basses hang back. Tympani tighten, and we've all agreed
to simply listen. Air conditioners

press upon us a Finnish winter breeze, then somewhere in the back
of my old lady's throat

I begin to worry about last winter's pneumonia: how I coughed,
how I leaked

in shame. Suppressing this cough makes me cough more, leaking
again. More horribly,

the rest of the concert I sit oddly warm in my teal velvet seat:
on through *En Saga's*

hurried violins, wave murmurs, the ripples of an idling outboard:
on through Sibelius' 7th Symphony:

the uncanny instant we choose to behave as adults as the solo oboe's
reed breaks wind mid-note:

on through Rachmaninoff's Piano Concerto in D Minor: played
by Lilya Ziberstein, a short,

middle-aged Russian, dressed in some shapeless gray affair,
but her hands intent, leaping

among her frothing notes, pebbles, gravel, rocks as her music splashes
over Ruth Eckerd's Steinway—

a glacial erratic, resting upon the shore—pouring through
the orchestra's myriad staves

until Clearwater's tough crowd gives her a ten minute standing
ovation while I, shrugging off disgrace,

tie my jacket around my waist, to rise for the last half
of Lilya's applause.

Alligator Regrets the Anhinga

Cold days sleep longer than the languorous
days of September. Not everything
about owning a lake requires
one to be above board.
                        Oh, quick, quick
see how the snake bird dives! Equality
appears to dwell in the air.

Anhinga. *Adult male: black with greenish
gloss...legs short, feet webbed. Stabs fish
in the side, flips it up to swallow headfirst.*

*Known for habit of swimming with just neck
and head above water.* Could have been my father.

Alligator. Alligator. Alligator. Everywhere
what's that splashing? Loose
child? Lost python? Do some dogs swim
faster than the shadows of fish? Taste is the least of it.

Alligator Orders the Animal Powers Meditation Kit

I hiss high summer, lie near
my lake's warm skin. Here I watch

Madre Maria where she nudged—no—piled
my lake's muck and last year's rushes.

There she shat small bones, hid
what is mine. I watch her pee

on that rush-covered mound, hiss
off crow, hankering 'coons, and me!

Does Maria remember how we met
at the north end of my lake,

how she turned a little to one side,
raised her tail? Forgot how I took

her 'round her belly, turned my tail
sideways and under her, how I felt?

Alligator Reasons a World View

My lake grows its own soft shoes
where land nurses water. Muck—
half silt, half rotted algae—
smiles 'round the shore.
Hush. Splash. Rile.
                  Subdue.
My lake thins, the bank lifts warm.
O hushed robe. Black
home on my belly: dozing, waiting.

Once, I dreamed the sunlight
                         changed,
shifted. Something slopped. Slid
near. Something pale blinked

a blue eye. Slid nearer alligator-like,
yawned its infinite-toothed grin.

When I awoke,
            I dreamed
Jose Blanco, the white alligator,
was black like me.
               I knew
all crows are black.
All shadows are dark.

Ledge

Up here in the low 70's, past puberty,
high school, most final exams, childbirth,
one failed marriage, menopause's heat,
and only three real jobs, how good it is
to forget, let the instant haze of memory
fill in my blues with a low static hiss
right down to the amount of dust
on my vital records. I nap
unashamed. I read books with no
social or literary value. I watch
movies on DVD's, pause for bath-
room breaks. Springs weaken.
Scale numbers fade. I don't try
anymore to be fair. I give random
presents. I parcel out my stuff
that makes me feel guilty: posed
photographs, crystal, toys, silk
flowers, dishes my mother
gave me that probably made her
feel guilty, too. But, who knows?
No one keeps track of what happens
up here on these ledges. From a distance
I must look like a hunched boulder.
Closer, you would see my spidery
veins writing narratives up and down
my legs as if I were a rendering
of a precarious Rosetta Stone. Mere
rubble or lost tax exemption or
a feast's proclamation—what my life
means I'll never know. I tend the coals
of *this* marriage in our house perched
on 80 loads of fill, though I still dream
dreams connecting my past to this morning's
sunrise overlooking the blank, granite
surface of our silent lake.

Aubade

First light. The murmur of thunder wakes me.

I watch you sleep, breathe. Your right hand trembles.
Good dreams or bad? (You claim you do not dream.)

You turn your back to me. Shift your pillow.
You sleep, breathe. Your right hand trembles.
The rain begins in green and yellow light.

You shift your pillow, turn back to me.
I wish I were the horse you ride into a dream.
The rain begins in green and yellow light.
You curl your arm around my graying head.

I am the horse you ride into your dream,
where every field you enter seems to overwhelm.
You brush your fingers through my graying hair.

Good dreams or bad, you claim we do not dream
when every field we enter leads to another realm:

fused light. A murmur of thunder wakes us.

Paraphasia

> —*a disturbance in verbal out put,*
> *a common dementia symptom involving substitution*
> *of letters in a word or substitution of one word for another*

Belle, my head is filled with gypsies,
stealing the hinges off my gate,
stealing graduate school, stealing ginger's
taste. No more cookies. No long glass
left. What's going on in my brain?
Birds, I guess.

You know what I mean. Don't guess
blackbirds again this morning. Those black gypsies
know everything I know—how my stains
grow dimmer, how my gate
swings both ways. Belle, where's my field glasses?
I can't find my champagne. Now, I'm all flat ginger

ale. Belle, pass my Aricept. Put a little ginger
in my step. Keep time waiting, I guess.
Take the smudges off my long glasses
now that the herons have returned. 'Spose the gypsies
lured them back with fish brains,
spilled my Intercept. Opened my heron's gate;

closed the off-switch on my seagull gate.
Touch on, touch off, touch the baby's ginger
hair. Gather your pains
while you may. Guess
our new granddaughter's name. Gypsy?
Tigna? Teagan? Belle, where's my glasses?

No, not those. I mean my long, black glasses,
the ones I used to see what the hawk ate
down by the lake. Better the hawk than those gypsies,
stealing every last morsel—ginger
and all. I know that. Maybe I guess.
Belle, what's happened to my grain?

Mind you, I used to own silos filled with grain.
Now, all I know is that my glass
is half empty. My guesses
are all half full. One gate
closes. Another opens for Teagan's ginger
hair—sea gulls, lake, and all my gypsies.

Inadmissible Evidence

He says.
She says.
He hears.
She hears.
He fears.
She believes.

She believes
he says
he fears.
She says
she hears.
He hears

he hears
she believes.
She hears
he says
she says
he fears.

He fears
he hears
she says
she believes
he says
she hears.

She hears
he fears
he says
she says
she believes
he hears.

He hears
she hears
she believes.
He fears
she says
he says

he says he hears.
She says she hears
his fears she believes.

Neutral Ground

I praise the wisdom of Switzerland.

I praise third wires, sewers, landfills—
those engineered discharges—carrying
our clutter back to the tender earth.

I praise The Society for the Prevention
of Blindness Thrift Shop. How else dispose
of things we can no longer bear,
though too dear to throw away?

I praise college dorms, hospitals,
city parks, safe deposit boxes
holding divorce decrees—those
places for lingering 'til our next turn.

I praise, however narrow, demilitarized
zones, boulevards, empty seats between
the aisle and window: fallow fields
dreaming of wild flowers.

Irretrievably Broken

At my ring's open cut, nothing again
ever will be equal.
                      One side shrinks
back under the law.
                          The other leans
forward toward grace.
                        One edge
shadowed metal: the other tarnished
silver:
      like last year's
river ice.

I know what I have tried to say.
I will never know what you have heard.

Relief

If there are six golden fish swimming
and a shark eats three, how many are left?
I praise the child who answers, "Where?"

I praise the order of fading bruises:
red, purple, blue, green, yellow,

and the professional bull rider
who says "You have to ride eight seconds
because them's the rules."

Some say the highest form of control
is knowing when to let go: praise
earthquakes, glaciers, and chunks
                              of thunder
breaking off. I praise *the ax for the frozen sea*.
Praise those who dine alone.

Praise the flying trapeze! Also vacations,
sabbaticals—all pilgrimages. Why return?

The Pastor's Ex-wife's Compline

> *He said to them, "For your hardness of heart Moses allowed you to divorce your wives, but*
> *from the beginning it was not so."*
> *—Matthew 19:8*

Ritual of bath,
lotion's silk gown,
Zocor, ibuprofen,

leftover king-size bed,

detective novel:
my ice water settles,
goes tepid

into The Great Silence.

Prayer for My Last Husband's New Wife

> *No mention shall be made of coral,*
> *or of pearls; for the price*
> *of wisdom is above rubies.*
>   *—Job 28: 18*

God! Help her.
Give her peace
where I found
none, patience when
he forgets he
forgot, a smile
when he farts.

God, keep her
strong when his
team loses and
just weak enough,
so he will
always win. Mea-
sure her whims;

for, so help me,
I no longer like
the wife
I became with
him. Bear my
prayer, this jewel
I have earned.

Selected Poems

*That I may raise and stand, o'rethrow me, and bend
Your force, to break, blow, burn, and make me new.
 Holy Sonnet XIV l 3,4
 John Donne*

Landscape with Six Plastic Flamingos

Like child birth, this crisis is of my own choosing
made one passionate Saturday morning six
days and nine months ago when words
alone were useless. My searching for
relief from the self's dictionary with another
has come to this nexus—a pink sestina—

though mid-labor it seems the sestina,
like a pick-up football team, has done the choosing.
Will they throw me the ball? Am I just another
skinny neighbor kid chosen because six
against seven are not enough for
a game? My team calls me Snake Lips, words

that hurt, because they're true. My words
slither around in the dream that is sestina,
a kind of pink story I make for
the man who landscapes with plastic flamingos, choosing
not art, he says, but what he likes. Six
constitutes his flamingo quorum—another

small scantling for maintaining another
sort of peace. His flamingos and my words
could be anywhere, curving out in six
directions, void and cold—the mind's sestina
a chaos. It's the glory of choosing, choosing
anything that frees and shapes us for

our lorn, featherless flight. I look for
words. They're sea shells—here's one, here's another—
fix, coral, rampion, charismatic, tame, wing—choosing
some for shape, some for sound. These words
toss, jostle, ping, loop, unravel until sestina
pinks them. They're integrated, six

flamingos browsing, no longer at sixes
and sevens, knees bent the wrong way for
humans, though just right for a sestina
about the mind's plastic shore: another
landscape of blood, salt, and words
that fancies pink, artificial birds choosing

flight—another sestina for six words' choosing.

Decoration Day

Driving to the cemetery with everything
you need for planting geraniums, you
hear the water slosh, the spade settle, and know
this grave gardening isn't
easy. The flowers are the wrong
color red, Aunt Martha tells you. *Honey*

we've always had magenta. Honey,
now turn left here, then right. Everything
seems confounding: your parents' graves on the wrong
side of the cemetery lane. You
haul the flowers and what water hasn't
spilled to where you know

your parents are, although you know
they will never know you are here. *Honey,*
look over there. George Whiteley wasn't
a veteran. Why's he got a flag? Everything
about this cemetery has gone downhill. You
follow Aunt Martha's instructions, move the wrong

flag to the right grave. *Poor Tom Brown, wrong*
again. Flunked out of school, you know.
Joined the navy just in time for Pearl Harbor. You
remember how he limped up your walk peddling honey
in bear-shaped jars and bees-wax candles—everything
sweet and warm—and how your mother wasn't

really smiling when she said, "Isn't
it good to see you again, Tom." Is it wrong
to think that way about your mother? Everything
about her seemed so clear, yet you know
sometimes she let things happen, like honey
left too long turning into sugar. You

plant what you now see are orange geraniums you
will abandon to their death, for this isn't
a cemetery with perpetual care. *Honey,*
I'll take these pots, so you won't buy the wrong
color again next year. You know
how your mother loved pink and rose everything.

Honey, turning right, then left isn't wrong.
Turn left after the gate. You know,
I can't thank you enough for everything.

Gong

> *Though I speak with the tongues of men*
> *and angels, and have not charity, I am become*
> *a sounding brass, or a tinkling cymbal.*
>   —*I Corinthians 13: 1*

I am what I am says the gong
not meaning to sound like chatter
of strangers near your soul's center
while fear of me follows where I go
like feathers disturbing your rest
and the brass-colored sky I have come

to believe is evening has come
a little too soon like a gong
left in the shivering wind to rest
while its maker stops to chatter
with postmen and angels who go
about their business and center

themselves in his light the center
that holds so fast I wish he's come
to finish what he began and go
with his copper-green hands from gong
to gong hammering our chatter
and our dimpling questions that rest

in rings like old trees giving rest
within their imperfect centers
to birds and squirrels that chatter
and churr their warnings when you come
too close to their homes rigged with gongs
hung from wrinkled limbs that go

to the trees' secret doors where stairs go
down through the roots to earth to rest
in the glimmering places where gongs
and water whisper the centers
of stories saving the ends to come
later around a fire's chatter

while poking the coals of old chatter
of what might have been if you'd go
not alone but together to come
though the rumoring thunder to rest
every night in the brass-bound center
of the mysterious laughter of gongs

False Aralia

My uncle says I look mean
in my fifth grade picture. Best
gray dress. Takes no shine to my lace
he says I used to hide my ugly neck.
It was hard to hold still—look false
so long—calm as Aunt Martha's aralia
plant. Used to be my Mom's aralia
she kept safe from mean
things. You know, dogs, spilled beer, false
moves. Strange plant. Does its best
in the shade. Holds its neck
straight wearing its quivering leaves like lace-
edged steak knives arranged upon a lace
cloth on a table near an aralia
and a few violets, stretching their necks
towards the sun where I didn't mean
to stumble over a rocking chair. Best
not to think about that sweet, false
laugh pinning me like a brooch to my lace
rag self. Swelled up finger thing busting
through my shadowed aralia
place all mean
wet shudder his hard breathing on my neck
where blood and air make my neck
a bridge between my false-
bottomed body and where my mean
thoughts after a while grow lacy
here on the porch by the aralia
that used to be my Mom's own best
place where she said she did her best
thinking. She'd smooth the neck
of her guitar, flick her cigarette past the aralia,
and seemed somehow to twist her false
notes into lace,
airy stuff that helps me think past meanness.

Kohl

> *When Jehu came to Jezreel, Jezebel heard of it; and she painted her eyes, and adorned her head, and looked out of the window. And as Jehu entered the gate, she said, "Is it peace, you...murderer of your master?" And he lifted up his face to the window, and said..."Throw her down" so they threw her down; and some of her blood spattered on the wall and on the horses, and they trampled on her.*
> —II Kings 9: 3–3

> *She piled up stones pretending they were home.*
> —"Kairos and Logos" W.H. Auden

There was a time before I called myself
a woman when I played about my father's
sun-lit temple, his temple's gong my mirror
of who I was. I had no use for paint
or power—these clawed hands were pretty pieces.
I piled up stones pretending they were home.

The god of rain and thunder was his mirror
of how one ought to mount the clouds of self
with neither pity nor shame. Baal was peace-
ful after the rains—as was my incensed father.
I piled up stones pretending they were home,
while he shrouded Baal's cedar hide with paint.

Between the desert and the sea, the piece
that fit was me. My purple sea this mirror:
I piled up stones pretending they were home.
Mounting my shadowed throne of self,
I conveyed commands, saw with these painted
eyes eight hundred priests multiplying Father.

They piled up stones, pretending they were home,
assembling my cedar Baal—each piece
of leg and horn and phallus painted
green, purple, gold—my dear Phoenician mirror
of how the desert seemed after Father
Thunder had sown our land with scattered self.

What color is these Jews' invisible paint?
They pile up stones pretending they are home
with their god, I Am, pretending he is father
in their stolen land of Canaan's pieces.
They've usurped Phoenician cedar for themselves,
festooned their tabernacle, their mirror

of what they claim their frightening father
made. Their laws are clever curses that paint
my desert with my husband's precious blood.
They pile up stones pretending god is home.
My kohl-edged eyes foresee beyond this mirror
a darkening window, my truths in pieces:

I piled up stones pretending they were home.
Now I paint my eyes before my father's mirror.
A seer glares through me. Is this my peace?

Courier

While my mother's heart waits for the medical courier
making his way along I-79, *Steal a look at the Erie Times—*
other drivers out of my way on this boring road. My bold
plans will keep my faded mother alive; at some point
life and death will merge with a part of Mom saved.
Happens all the time—damn trucks ridin' my ass up the landscape.

Other 'n drivin' this tin can, what can I do? Landscape
while the sun fries my brains? Shovel McDonalds? Courier
Life Services—join the crew! I'm all mapped out, saved,
making trips from Pittsburgh to read the Erie Times—
happens to be what I do. Who should I call? At some point
plans will have be arranged: funeral, her apartment—the bold

lifestyle Senior Meadows promised—erased. What was bold
(other than her tiny east facing balcony she landscaped)
happened to be her heart she gave too readily at any point
while Father kept his hidden and closed. "The courier
plans his breaks around the eye and heart's degeneration times,
makes sure the carry vessel's contents are carefully saved"

happens to suck. When do I take a leak? Travelin' lifesaver
seeks relief at local roadside pickle park. Only bold-ass
planners need apply. Hope no old lady's here this time.
Other than her bruised arm when she returned from landscape/
life class last week (fell at the rest stop, said some courier
while hurrying bumped her), nothing kept her from her paint:

planned 39 scenes of French Creek winding south. "Some point
happens where the creek bends, and the moving light I've saved
makes my heart stop," Mom said. "The creek is just the courier;
life is best composed with that light, uncertain though bold,
while French Creek disappears beyond a curving landscape."
Other than her art and me, her only child, will the *Erie Times*

make the tie-in between her bruise and her stroke? *Every fuckin' time
plans get screwed by lugging hearts from point to point
while being paid the minimum.* Maybe Mom was right: landscape
happens in the art of looking sideways. Nothing keeps us safe.
Others might wish she had a more profound or bolder
life's ending than simply giving way to an ironic courier.

The Dynamite Maker's Mistress

A very small, but not bad, soul is hidden in you.
  —Alfred Nobel
  from a letter to his mistress, Sophie Hess,
  written shortly before his death

The man I failed at loving well is dead. Small
memories come and go though not
release, as if he still owns me like a bad
dream: at Heaven's gate I greet his soul:
Alfred? You...here? His red beard almost hides
his grin. He says, *It was the nitroglycerin*

that staled. Like me, he says his nitroglycerin
tablets let him down every day in small
ways. If that is Heaven, where can I hide?
I wake, arise, sip my water, cannot
afford the sherry that numbed my soul
those sullen nights during those other bad

affairs. Was I naive or just bad,
expecting every day to be like nitroglycerin—
an oily clarity—that might explode my soul
to kingdom come upon the small
counterpane of courtship, French-knotted
like the white heads of dandelions hiding

from the scythe? I hear the leaves falling, hiding
with their white sound the rough beat of my bad
heart. Angina flickers down my arm, though not
that orange tightening that only nitroglycerin
can loosen. These pale tablets, so small
they're almost motes, hold my soul

paused beneath my tongue. "Soul,"
they say, "stay! O taste and see. Hide
not your self from either dreams or the small
failures of unmade beds, dust, or bad
coffee." This, of course, is a lot for nitroglycerin
or any other god to say, though not

as much as my first lover promised. (Not
that I believed him...well, some.) My soul
is an easy believer—wishbones, nitroglycerin,
any chant, daily horoscopes permeate my hide.
These autumn days I tire of disbelief. Bad
arteries my doctor blames for my heart's small

troubles, not my sherry. Tonight, I hide
my soul's failures and my heart's bad
choices, trusting again this small medicine.

Hosea Three

> *When the Lord first spoke through Hosea,*
> *the Lord said to Hosea, "Go take to yourself a wife of harlotry and have*
> *children of harlotry...." So he went and took Gomer,*
> *the daughter of Diablaim, and she conceived and bore him a son.*
>
> *...for I am God and not man...*
> —*Hosea 1: 2,3; 11: 9b*

Gomer

Am I nothing more than a slippery hole for
you? I have been appointed to be what I am—
anyone's lover. If you remove what god
has given me—my smile, my tender curls, and
easy nakedness—your scrabbling hands, not
my fingers, will shrivel, dry as your man-

hood dried last night and again this morning. Man,
against your will I feel you swell and ease for
Yahweh who made you—like me—lower, not
equal with his airy angels. I am
your land: your hills, your shadowed valley, and
your story. Tell me. You love your god

who loosens the rain when he will, your god
who shut the Red Sea's doors upon the men
of obedient Egyptian women and
their swaddled, unnamed babies for
your amazement's sake. Why should your great I Am
blame you for loving me? Though I'm cursed, I'm not

as cold-blooded as he. Heed: *Cast me not*
away from your presence, restore, O God,
the joy of your salvation. If I am
your joy (I've heard you moan like other men),
uphold me now with your freed spirit, for
I quiver like a lost bird from Egypt, and

a new child settles in me as ill-named and
ill-fathered as my others. I cannot
help that I love babies, men, or you; for
I have been made adulterous by your god,
his own loose metaphor, confusing man
about the cords of freedom and love. I am

the one you sent away—you loved me, and
you feared the others would know. Poor man,
is there insufficient love for all? You'll not
sleep alone in the milk-filled land your god
has given everyone. Take me back, for

God's sake, I am a woman and not a man.

Hosea

Have I been sent to plow the eastern wind for
You again? My words are chaff when I am
near her. Your laws crumble in my mouth. O God,
how can I speak for you? She melts my words and
turns them into stories. Her fingers, not
Your judgement, entangle my fringed garment. Man

was not made for woman; she was made for man.
I know the laws of Deuteronomy, for
You have written: *Her former husband may not
again take her to be his wife.* (I am
assured of her defilement!) Her bones and
her lovers' dust shall lie unburied in God's

promised land. Bring down the goatherd gods
that haunt the springs in her pleasured valley. Men
like me have heard their mourning doves and
languished, been filled with strange hungers for
her cloven idols and lawless ways. I am
the one whose words proclaimed the Lord's law, not

faithless love. You, Lord, are jealous, though not
of valleys. I entered Gomer's hollows, god-
less. That woman of raisin cakes! I was
enslaved by her Egyptian ways—unmanned
when she serviced other men. I loved her for
the shadowed valleys between her breasts and....

She is no longer my wife! She turned away and
slipped into a wilderness. I shall not
search her paths. End her feasts, her laughter, for
she has consorted with other men, other gods,
scorned Your laws that made her my woman.
Banish her sweets and incense—I am

a cup of vinegar mixed with gall. Am I
to be defiled by Your demanding counsel and
cast away by both love and law? A gray man,
sifting my grain from smoke and dung, a naught,
bartering back my life's sorrow? O God,
I tremble. Fill me with Your right words, for

I am not a woman's but God's man.

Yahweh

Do I dine on cakes and miracles for
breakfast? Can I see how perfect I am
while sprinkling poppies through your God-
filled barley fields, sailing thistle seeds and
purple birds through your groves of olives not
simply for my pleasure but so any man,

walking through a garden with a woman
in the evening may ignore a loose thread for
a moment hanging from my garment? Not
that her words are flowers, but that I am
hidden in her eyes, in her circling stories, and
in her womb. Would you unravel God?

Who hardened Pharaoh's heart beyond his gods'
best gryphon reason: half lion's, half man's
dumb metaphor between flummery and
speculation? Who lit the sapphire for
the sake of my blue-shadowed feet? I am
in the bee's sting and in her honey. I'm not

a dulled harvest knife—though you'll not
be dispossessed of grinding stones. Is God
alone in silence: an unsaid prayer? I am
the one who sought companionship with men—
shared bread upon that cloud-clapped mountain for
mine and Moses' amazement—and

then how soon you haggled over written and
unwritten love down in your valleys. No
stars I knew then were faint or absent, for
the truth is that I was lonely. Your God
is both mountain and clearing, enticing man
for a moment to enter the light I am.

You wonder if the invitation I am
extending is a constant question and
if I know your choices before you do. Man
nor woman is ever fully known (not
for lack of searching) in the valleys God
clears each morning of mist and shadows, for

I am God and neither man nor woman.

At the Corner of Hoover and Sparkleberry

*Live your life as a bourgeois that you
may be violent and original in your art.*
—Gustave Flaubert

I need a fix.
    Here among the coral-
        trimmed houses safe from rampion
            cravings, filth, or charismatic
                plots, the past is a tame
                    account told by a parrot, wings

                clipped. *Wings? What wings?*
he squawks. He's fixed:
                saved from buffalo sauce—hot or tame—
    oily coral
        smothering possibilities of charismatic
    marjoram or rampion

        desire. You know the tale: how rampion
                led to Rapunzel's tower, her wings—
    her tumbling charismatic
hair—her prince a quick fix
    in the lonely forest's coral
        suburbs. Pretty tame

            unless you happen to be the witch. Tame
    was loss: her walled garden's rampion,
    her bartered daughter's coral
            lips. (Who cares which lips?) Wings,
kisses, a pretty perch fixed
        that witch's charismatic

        soul. Is my charismatic
            soul (well, character) too tame?
Has the art of fixing
        shadowed lines with words—my rampion
                desire—taken wing,
    left for some exotic island's coral

       reef, self-maimed amid the coral
              sunsets like some charismatic
                     Gauguin? For years invention's wings
                  hopped, stuttered, stooped on the tame
           beach at Kitty Hawk until rampant
desire took off, provided the fix.

Mahjongg

And the crack in the tea-cup opens
A lane to land of the dead.
             —W. H. Auden

Am I wasting my time Wednesday mornings
with the Mahjongg ladies, laughing as we crack
our luck, gathering patterns of flowers
and dots from among the seasons and winds?

Outside, real birds sing. Inside, dragons
rear, clack among these old, ivory tiles.
Bamboo's ceaseless growth stalls here with flowers,
racked and counted like mugs of morning

tea set out for sale on a dragon-
haunted street. I've uncovered a crak,
like a load of snow slipping from the tiles
of a steep roof. I've caught three kongs of winds—

4 east, 4 west, 4 south—and saved a pair of dragons,
thrown out my dots, then sacrificed my flowers

for Mahjongg! I ponder my lucky tiles,
wonder if skill could account for a morning
like this: a sun-filled room, Rose, Evie, and Dee's winding
and unwinding of their families' lives:
                              A cracked
tooth and just some soreness when Mom fell on that tiled
floor." "*All year long played Dungeons and Dragons*
until his dad marched up there, took the wind
out of his sails." "*Made Dean's list, sent me flowers*
to celebrate." "*My Jim's smile and then his mind cracked,*
crumbled like a sand castle 'til...he slept away."
                              Morning
shifts to cake and sugarless tea. Outside, the wind
stills, our hands touch as we stir the tiles,
erect our brief walls. East discards a crak.

Pursuing my bamboos, I cast out a dragon.
Am I the missionary, this morning,
my mother wanted me to be? Flowers

thrive on this Chinese wall, curtain my cracking
faith that anything is likely: a wind—
sudden, God-sent—might take me up this morning;

show me my life, arranged like Mahjongg tiles
in fragile walls, replay me like a flower
so hybrid it never seeds. Dragons

might rage among these tiles, the four winds
scatter earth's imagined flowers. My dragons,
though, dance this morning to the call of ivory's crack.

Janet Reno's Poinciana Tree

*Sitting on a couch in her office, where the picture
of a poinciana tree stands like a family photo on her desk,
Janet Reno spoke affably...about the pressure of this moment.*

Trees stand aloof from us in possession, like
relatives, of their own memories:
photos of bark and branches they
affably want to show us at the wrong
moment. For us to understand how
pressure of holding an entire field in their grasp,

pressure of tracing a human mind in the air makes
trees ungainly, we must put aside our flowering
moments, those times we think were most graceful
relative to weather or politics. We must efface the time we
affably chaired a personnel committee, provided
photocopies of a friend's failures. We must destroy our icy

photographs of a woman's grief taken under
pressure of *evidence is where you find it.*
(Affability made those liberties easier.)
Trees, though, extend their trembling branches in
relative address to anyone willing
momentarily to enter their rooted dimensions:

momentarily to regard whispered small words;
photos of hawks in their appointed homes; their
relative deprivations—those tensions of *ought* and *is*—
pressures that even poinciana
trees carry. Their trembling, scarlet flowers,
affably edged with yellow remain

ineffable, though flashy for months when
moments of splendor are all that most of us can bear.
Photos seem unnecessary when one lives with a poinciana
tree, the same way we fail to preserve a prying
relative on film. Our aunt's heart attack provides
pressure—a feeble tourniquet against life's ever

pressuring questions. We try, of course, to be
affable, say something about our new camera to this
relative who now is vaguely quiet, while we regret those
moments we set aside her curiosities—
photos of her neighbor's yard governed by a poinciana
tree, her musings about Janet Reno in the *New York Times.*

The Pastor's Wife Considers Her 57th Birthday

I'm no Molly Bloom, but I'll say yes
    to another year
        of choir practice, tea, gossip of yeast
            infections, recycled paper, yard
                work, committees, pious smiles, yarn,
                    gelatin salads, and waiting for Yahweh

                to come again with prime-time news. Yahweh,
I've said yes and yes and yes
        to the tangled yarn
    of congregation and parsonage. These years
        of planting pear trees in someone else's yard
    have grown a sort of longing, a yeast

    of expectation, that your Spirit's yeast
        in your recipe for me would be revealed. Yahweh,
    of cubits, of multiples of 40 yards,
take my measure. Say in that ancient delicate way, *Yes,*
woman, with whom it has ceased after fifty seven years
    to be as it is with women, take yarn,

        take heart, take—here I unravel like the yarn
    of worn sweaters. How can I speak for Yeast
when all I have are these factorless years?
            How can I know the slow explosions of Yahweh?
Still, I wish for a champagne yes,
    one not uttered by me in my borrowed yard

    that's no more mine than any yard
        belongs to those knitting the yarn
of holy time, those who've said yes
    when angels, whirl winds, fire, or yeast-
        less bread spoke for Yahweh.
I count my print-dressed years—

    those bundled seasons turned to years—
        shared in the congregation's house and yard
          with a man more Yahweh's
            than mine. All his flowers are tied with the yarn
    of love's duty, and yet like yeast
he rises, loves me...well, and thoroughly, and shouts, *Yes.*

Four Residents

Apple Hearts for Sylvia Plath

I am learning how to play
    Hearts
        on a computer
            here at The Residence. My Dad
                does not approve
                    of playing cards.

                Winning is hard
this spring. I try to find a way
            to soothe
my fears of losing heart,
            trampling layers of leaves Dad
    laid down like a computer

        over my decomposing infrastructure:
        my understory that Dad
        hardly
bothers to tell me anymore. "Apples," he'd say,
        don't move
far from the tree." to keep me a part

    of his western Pennsylvania heart
where gypsy moths and rust corrupt
        my mind's economy—"Conserve,
            win, spade
longer" (though not deeper), get your way."
                    In this new game at the end

            of each hand
you get one point for each heart,
13 for the Queen of Spades. The way
        you lose is if you win 100 points or
            if the dealer quits the game. Above
        all, discard

>   high cards,
>   by taking inessential hands. (Dad
>   would never approve.)
>   To win, take all the hearts
>   and the Queen of Spades, like a computer
> executing *delete* gone fey.
>
> Somewhere, Sylvia, play all your cards from your heart
>   against your Daddy's approval.
> Shoot the moon with computer apples—play!

Getting up, Leaving

I go to movies,
    not films. Things are strange
        enough here at The Residence
            without Fellini
                running up and down the stairs. We make
                our own art.

                Tuesday's art
class is usually held in the sunny space
        over the garage, encouraged by the lady
    giving out lace, feathers, string,
        knives. Evelyn
            is careful to say, "Tell me

            about it." I try to stay with lace...
but my father never chopped
    off chickens'
heads. "Don't like all that fuss,
        and they don't bleed enough," he'd say while
hanging them up by their yellow-scaled

    claws with their blood conveniently
        rushing to their beaks.
            He'd slip his father's jackknife's longest blade
                up their mouths—twisting
twice—their iridescent
    flapping, slowing like trains

    in grainy European films.
Then, "That's good."

Hats, Fans, Coffins, Boats

While settling my molecules, what if
    all I ever do at The Residence
        is make baskets? How do I finish
            the tangled turnings
                around my unraveling raffia core
                      that the art lady says comes from Madagascar?

                Alluvial depressions form Madagascar's
upland plains like scattered baskets, as if
    their raffia cores
were intermittently sewn by residents,
        mindlessly wandering, turning
useless, and unfinished.

    Hats, fans, coffins, and boats remain unfinished
            for their use on my Madagascar's
        western shore, turning
among the groves of raffia palms as if
    this island's residents
             were unraveling at their core.

        What am I at my very core?
    Just a message each firing synapse finishes,
    or a collection of genes governed by residency—
            an island like Madagascar,
detached by continental drift? What if
    I'm an incompetent turner

        adding lengths to myself, called to turn
            about my core
of self, a sort of
        angst machine forever brooding and unfinished?
No! I'd rather be a basket in Madagascar
to be used every day for steaming rice, a residence

fashioned so well (unlike The Residence),
I would serve unnoticed. My every turn
would hold in Madagascar
enough rice to feed a child's core,
so that daily a hungry child might finish
all her rice without considering *if*.

Letter Home

Dear Ben, I share a bathroom—
    claw foot tub, jury-rigged shower,
        a marble thing more
            font than sink,
                and a toilet.
                      Sometimes I have to listen.

                Here at The Residence, listening
determines where we room,
            medication, and if they let
us read the newspaper or shower
        alone. Insistent voices sink
your ship. Less is more

    privileges. More
            or less listening
is about right, though bathroom
        jokes can become a Freudian sink:
            A slip of the tub—healthy humor—toilets
send you to the showers.

    Hearing Lisa shower
        early this morning seemed more
            normal than the wait for her flushing toilet.
            I caught myself listening
        to the on and off of the sink
as if you—naked—were rinsing your razor in our bathroom

at home. Something stirred. Fell. Lisa's bathroom—
    no sharps allowed—shower,
        toilet,
      sink—
    wrong order! I opened our door to more
        blood and pills than I have ever dreamed, listened

                      to Lisa's crumpled breathing, listened
to myself whisper *no*. Our bathroom
      all morning has been a flurry—more
and more inspections of the shower,
           the cleansing of the marble sink,
                    the centering of suspicion on the toilet.

            Ben, that meteor shower in my mind has sunk
                  below my horizon. Once more, I want to listen,
if you'll let me, to your mornings in our bathroom.

Perchance, Each Interstate

Rising like a plastic sack in traffic
    wind, chance seems to take
        on a life of its own. At the verge
            it skitters, is sucked back, dreams.
              Is what keeps a sack playing
                  the belief things will get better?

            Or, no victim, does a plastic sack take
    her chances, skip over the verge,
cross six lanes of traffic,
        chase her half-filled dreams—
            silk, foreign perfumes, better
            wine—into a dark wood where foxes play?

        By happenstance, one of the thousands of dreamers
    passing today may stop on a verge,
        overwhelmed while a song playing
  on his car radio takes
            him, empties his sack of grief. Better,
lighter, he re-enters the traffic.

    What if lying in a sack on a verge
unnoticed by the heavy traffic
        is the crumpled chance on a dream,
            say, a little girl's play
house? A road crew, prison worker takes
            it, wins. Will his winning make things better?

        Refuge and prospect are at play
    with the odds when a plastic sack takes
flight in chancy traffic.
            No one knows that better
        than the driver who glimpses—not dreams—
    a motorcyclist shoeless, face down on the verge.

               Perchance, Milton Samuel, Mary Better,
         Beno Fishback, Ross Maxwell, or Vergie
Walton are today's members of the interstate traffic
                   who may follow a plastic sack as it plays
      across their path, dances, takes
                   over like the voice that narrates their dreams.

The Pastor's Wife Considers the Retirement of Fred the Magician

On the occasion of amateur magician, Dr. Frederick Reiz's retirement as President of Lutheran Theological Southern Seminary

How did you know when the magic
of serving had become mere slight of hand?
How will we discern that moment when we may
glaze our indeterminate work—
portraits of the Creator's eyes at rest
upon His systematics

of rivers, draining our seemingly systematic
sins into His sea of grace? Fred, your magic
tricks through the years have rested
on the precept that the hand
is slower than the eye. What the soul may
believe is not always the works

it sees, but rather what works
its way through the heart systematically.
Your slowed misdirections may
lead us to accept—wafer-like—the magic
coins you produce from you pockets to hand
to the poor cynic resting

inside each of us. The rest
becomes the Spirit's work.
Some days your patter faltered, your hands
loosened amid the fluttering systematics
of silken scarves. Though the meringue of your magic
made the horizons limitless, your retirement may

have rent some uncanny rule, may
have leapt past your imagination. You rest,
like me, within your own illusions. Your magic
persists in the forever unfinished work
of *kairos* and the systematic
manifestations of aces and veiled bouquets. One hand

palms a hollowed ball, while the other hand
appears empty. Your right hand may
twice stroke an invisible drape systematically.
With your third stroke you grasp the silk resting
in the hidden ball. You slowly work
a trinity of scarves from your empty hand. Fred, all magic

may rest in the revelation of Yahweh's works,
His systematics, freely carried out by our slight hands.

Elegy for Anthony Hecht

Who would have hoped for this eventual peace?
—"Green: an Epistle" Anthony Hecht

There's no facile way to console
    those of us mourning on this day,
        you, Dr. Hecht, who have forever annexed rot
           and all its possibilities. Your ivory
              bones slept in a mean tower
                fragile as the paper

                    you wrote your poems upon, those paper
lanterns of infinite folds, your ornamental consolations,
        cataloging Europe's towering
    losses—*The Hard Hours*, Yolek's day—
        now made into our grief, too. Yolek's ivory
    smoke falls upon us. We smell his rot,

        because you encountered rot
                in exquisite places, confronted paper
        with your lance—an ivory
iambic line. Such elegant consolation
you gave for your insufficient days
        amid the towering

snows of Rochester and the towering
    demands of the Dover bitch. Rot,
  after all was your key note, your day
            star enkindling your lines across paper.
I wonder what consolations
      you made of lymphoma, your very fluids' ivory

        betrayal? May you be met by an ivory
           being, Noh Ting Wong, a vast leaning tower
of an angel, an imperfect consoler
    (*misericord*, if you will) your guide through the rot
           of Heaven. Isaiah will explicate his paper
  reeds by the brooks. Horace will lend you his day

       bed where he so often lay
                with divers nymphs upon an ivy
                        counterpane to sip peppered
                    wine. And may the powers
             of Babel spread before you the whole lot
of a new, broken language—oh, glorious desolation!

A Cadenza for Arnaut Daniel

The invention of the sestina is usually attributed to Arnaut Daniel (fl. 1190)
   —The Princeton Encyclopedia of Poetry and Poetics

This time with my writing hand I enter
your words, Arnaut, leach through your fingernails,
slip into your six-sided mind to tap your soul.
(My fear is almost a nuclear rod—
so much potential.) I remember my uncle
drunk, his fumbling into a chamber

a bullet; I heard the click of an empty chamber,
felt his spit hissing, *Bitch*, heard him enter
another. Yes, you were right to choose *uncle*.
Did you touch with your thumb each fingernail,
too, counting your syllables out, the rod
of each line making and breathing your soul?

Warily, I examine your word, *soul*,
ashamed mine might be a vacant chamber
or worse—penciled where cliche has trod.
You wrote of a soul's persistence. I enter
your song of pain and devotion—nails
and all—a part of your ordinary of uncle

and sister, candle and night. My uncle
could be absolved, a few prayers free his soul.
These many years I have preserved him, nailed
in memory, though sealed in death's chamber.
What if I just forgot him? Would he enter
heaven or hell unchanged by plea or rod?

Why not let oblivion be his rod?
I'll strand him nameless like the uncle
who threatened your love, who entered
your poem but left unknown; for now my soul
follows your words into your chamber,
the poem you built with your heart and fingernails.

Holding my pen, circled by my fingernails,
I write these lines across your words, your *rods*,
my candles, as I wander your chamber's
maze. I greet your love, nod to your uncle's
dark ways. I find the portal where your soul
must have sometimes rested, then entered:

Nola sends her song of the uncle-nail
for the pleasure of Arnaut, her rod when soul
and honor enter sestina's chamber.

About the Author

Nola Garrett is Faculty Emerita of Edinboro University of Pensylvania. She presently lives in Downtown Pittsburgh, PA. She has received a Residency at Yaddo; Scholarships from White River Writers' Workshop, Bread Loaf Writers' Conference, West Chester Poetry Conference; and is listed on the Mezzo Cammin Women Poets Timeline. Her poems are posted on *The Georgia Review's Vault* and her monthly blog/essays are available online at Autumn House Press coalhillreview.com.

This is Nola's second book with Mayapple Press; *The Pastor's Wife Considers Pinball* was published in 2013.

Other Recent Titles from Mayapple Press:

Amanda Reverón, tr. Don Cellini, *El Silencio de las Horas / The Silence of the Hours*, 2016
    Paper, 70pp, $15.95 plus s&h
    ISBN 978-936419-67-8

Toni Mergentime Levi, *White Food*, 2016
    Paper, 82pp, $15.95 plus s&h
    ISBN 978-936419-65-4

Allison Joseph, *Mercurial*, 2016
    Paper, 42pp, $13.95 plus s&h
    ISBN 978-936419-64-7

Jean Nordhaus, *Memos from the Broken World*, 2016
    Paper, 80pp, $15.95 lus s&h
    ISBN 978-936419-56-2

Doris Ferleger, *Leavened*, 2015
    Paper, 64pp, $15.95 plus s&h
    ISBN 978-936419-47-0

Helen Ruggieri, *The Kingdom Where No One Keeps Time*, 2015
    Paper, 80pp, $15.95 plus s&h
    ISBN 978-936419-55-5

Jan Bottiglieri, *Alloy*, 2015
    Paper, 82pp, $15.95 plus s&h
    ISBN 978-936419-52-4

Kita Shantiris, *What Snakes Want*, 2015
    Paper, 74pp, $15.95 plus s&h
    ISBN 978-936419-51-7

Devon Moore, *Apology from a Girl Who Is Told She Is Going to Hell*, 2015
    Paper, 84pp, $15.95 plus s&h
    ISBN 978-1-936419-54-8

Sara Kay Rupnik, *Women Longing to Fly*, 2015
    Paper, 102pp, $15.95 plus s&h
    ISBN 978-1-936419-50-0

Jeannine Hall Gailey, *The Robot Scientist's Daughter*, 2015
    Paper, 84pp, $15.95 plus s&h
    ISBN 978-936419-42-5

Jessica Goodfellow, *Mendeleev's Mandala*, 2015
    Paper, 106pp, $15.95 plus s&h
    ISBN 978-936419-49-4

For a complete catalog of Mayapple Press publications, please visit our website at *www.mayapplepress.com*. Books can be ordered direct from our website with secure on-line payment using PayPal, or by mail (check or money order). Or order through your local bookseller.